A Boy to a Man

CHARLES MORTON

PAGE PUBLISHING
Conneaut Lake, PA

First originally published by Page Publishing 2024

ISBN 979-8-89157-402-1 (pbk)
ISBN 979-8-89157-421-2 (digital)

Printed in the United States of America

INTRODUCTION

This journey starts as a youth growing up in the inner city of Washington, DC. I witnessed my life transform from a boy to a man overnight. Growing up, I considered myself a gifted and talented child. My favorite subject was math, and as I got older, I would understand why. My mother did the best she could as a young mom of two. Her work skills were limited at the time, but she provided the best she could for her two children. In most of the inner-city households, there was not a male figure in the house. So like many, I was raised by women. My grandmother gave me an understanding of what it was to be a strong Black woman. She had seven children, and she loved each and every one of them dearly. I would witness her getting ready for work when I got out of school. She worked the night shift. For extra money, she would babysit. That only gave her less than eight hours of rest, but she made it work. She always made sure she cooked dinner before going to work. She used to be so tired coming home from work. I used to try my best to stay up to greet her coming through the door. She would always smile at me, then say, "Get your butt to bed." She used to call me her little man, and as I got older, I would understand my nickname and why.

CHAPTER 1

From the early ages of six to seven years old, I moved to Caroline County, Virginia, with my great-great aunt and uncle. To this day, I do not know why. Yes, my mother could not handle two children at once. I never asked her the reason. Being with them taught me life skills at an early age. This was the early eighties; there was no running water in the house. We had a wood stove for heating and cooking. There was an outhouse for a bathroom. At night, we used a bucket to take care of our needs. Everything I write is true.

We ate from the land, meaning they had chickens, pigs, and other animals. They had a smoke house to keep the meat from spoiling. They made the best out of anything. My aunt canned vegetables during the summertime from her garden that my uncle maintained for her. Of course, I had to help out around the house. Remember I was only six years old. My job was to help my uncle out with whatever he needed help with. A true hustler. The man for real. I then noticed I started getting strong. I had me carrying five-gallon buckets filled with water from the will outside. He had me loading wood into a wheelbarrow from trees he cut down. That was a hustle people did to make money before winter would hit. Most people had wood stoves. We would go fishing to catch hearings (fish) when they were in season. People would pay $50 for a five-gallon bucket of them, more if you sold them already cleaned. Cleaning was my job as well, the icing on the cake for someone my age. I was even helping to dig graves for people to be buried in.

Money was tight, but we managed. We had clean clothes to wear and food to eat. My grandmother's uncle moved in with us. He had diabetes real bad, so they cut off one of his legs. I think my mother let him move with us to help out with the bills. Before he lost one of his legs, he was a driver. Long before Lyft and Uber today, he used to drive people from the Safeway near Potomac Avenue Southeast. Since he lost his leg, he needed someone to help him with the groceries for his passengers, loading and unloading the groceries in and out of the car. So every few days of the week, I would ride with him. He always had me back before it got too late because I still had school in the morning. He would always drop knowledge on me, like "Don't spend all your money you make overnight" and "Always bring something back to the household when you come back." So every time I came back, I would have a carton of eggs, bacon, bread, milk, and juice. It might not seem like a lot, but for a child my age, it was. My uncle was teaching me to be a man. Today I give thanks to both my uncles for the knowledge they instilled in me at a young age. With my earnings, I would buy bags of candy from the candy lady around my way for my classmates. Teachers always asked where I got them. I would say I work with my uncle sometimes. They used to smile and praise my work ethic at my age. I would say I had a normal childhood. I played sports sometimes at the recreation center in my neighborhood, but I was always curious about everything. When I graduated from elementary school, my journey began. My first year of junior high school was a changing phase. In this book, some would say it was not normal at all.

When they say Southern folks are more seasoned than city folks, they are not lying. I was getting many lessons in life and did not realize it. Both passed away, but I will never forget them. I moved back with my mother when I was eight years old. I was starting the third grade.* So every time I came back, I would have a carton of eggs, bacon, bread, milk, and juice. It might not seem like a lot, but for a boy my age, it was. My uncle was teaching me to be a man. Today I give thanks to both of them for the knowledge they have instilled in me at a young age. With my earnings, I would buy bags of candy from the candy lady around my way for my classmates. Teachers always asked where I got the money, and I would say I worked with my uncle sometimes. They used to smile and praise my work ethic at my age. I would say I had a normal childhood. I played sports sometimes at the recreation center in my neighborhood, but I was always curious about everything. When I graduated from elementary school, my journey began. My first year of junior high school was my changing phase. In this book, some would say it was not normal at all.

I went to school but was not interested. I started selling drugs from weed and PCP to crack cocaine. My neighborhood was an open drug market. I did not take my skills seriously until years later. I was only twelve years old at the time. As long as I dressed nicely and had money in my pocket, I was good. In my second year of junior high school, I barely went. My mother thought I was going but I was not. Once I thought she was long gone, I would come back home. Parents at the time were smoking crack. My mother never was on hard drugs, and she did not mind working a job. I considered myself the man of the house. The bills were not crazy high as they are today. It really was not any stress on me. She did not have to worry about food, and I always bought things off the street. The only person she had to worry about was my younger brother. My mother was never a fan of what I did. I always gave my mother the respect she deserved. I never sold anything in her presence. I was not raised that way from my mother or grandmother. Sometimes she would ask about the goods I was bringing home. At the end of the day, she knew what I was doing. Just think about it, a twelve-year-old buying his own clothes.

I started getting in trouble more and more. I was headed down a road that would cost me dearly.

By the age of fourteen to fifteen years old, I had been at every juvenile facility in the city. Looking back, I put my mother through a lot growing up. That woman was always there for me no matter what. My grandmother was her ride-or-die. Both of them never turned their backs on me for anything. Deep down, they knew my self-worth. I guess you can say I was the special one. I was my grandmother's favorite. I could never do wrong in her eyes. They traveled many times to see me as a juvenile and adult.

My mother used to say some things that cut deep. She wanted me to change my ways to see where I was headed. Sometimes I cannot believe I am still here. God has a plan for me. Everything I was taught early on helped me and shaped me into the man I am today. What does not kill you makes you stronger. One has a story to tell that is why I am taking the time to write this book. It is a book about a man who finally wakes up and understands his purpose in life. Never give up and be thankful to see another day. As I go on, you will understand this is coming from my heart. You will feel my pain and understand the struggles of a Black man in America. You only know what was taught.

CHAPTER 2

I can remember every time one of us ran from or came back to the juvenile facility in Oak Hill. They had a list of everybody who graduated—that is what the councils called it anyway—being charged as an adult or those who were killed. Nobody wanted to see the name of a close friend that got killed. The councils did that to try and save the ones they could. Crack cocaine was taking over every city in America. During the year 1989, there were a lot who came in as boys but left as men back then. Many of us graduated or got killed. I was on the run from a group home I got sent to. At this point, I was a lost soul. I started smoking weed and drinking with a childhood friend of mine named Bugg. He and I would smoke and drink all the time. Even before, it was called thug passion. May he rest in peace.

Honestly, I really liked being a loner. I do not know why but I did. I always did my own thing and also loved being around the underdogs—the ones who thought they were someone and, years later, wanted to be around me. True story, I was always a likable dude with a huge heart and learned love can get you killed. Now that I was on the run, I could not stay at my mom's house. The police may pop up at any time. So I stayed on the move and did what I did to get money. One day, I was planning on getting some money.

I ran into a neighborhood friend, who was on the same mission as well. One thing led to another. Months later, I was in DC jail for second-degree murder. I was charged as an adult, yet I was seventeen years old at the time. That is when my life changed. I was facing fifteen years to life imprisonment, no more going to group homes or Oak Hill, just the juvenile block of the jail. One was facing the same charge or charges as well. My being young and dumb to the system cost me. I took a plea offer to a lesser charge. It was manslaughter, and it took five to fifteen years. My lawyer press me into this plea? I was not sure about my codefendant, just being honest. Never did he throw me under the bus—honestly, I can say that. They charged me and my codefendant was a free man after that experience. Never did I have another codefendant and always had a paid lawyer.

They moved me to Lorton. This time I was eighteen years old, and this was not a playground either. Real-lifers or men were doing a lot of time. They sent me to big Lorton, which was called the hill. I was one of the youngest from my hood there. It was me, myself, and I. Early lessons in life molded me to be aware of games. What is better than a game is more game. A few good men I did time with and juvenile facilities were there as well. It is sad to say, but I have been doing time so long that it is another level of it.

When I was at Oak Hill, they called it baby Lorton, but this was the real deal. I was eighteen years old, and my mother and grandmother were my support system. My so-called friends or other family members or girls I was dealing with at the time did not know anything about me doing time with anyone. Before long, I adjusted well, saying what happens in Lorton stays in Lorton. I saw a lot of shit being there. Another good childhood friend came to the hill. I called him Freak. Freak and I used to be together every day. I let Freak know everything was going on so he would be on point. Lorton was like the streets. Money makes the world go around. I was on moves, on all moves to get a dollar. Like I said, Lorton was like the streets. Real talk, you could get damn near anything you wanted. Your money was right; you were good. They started sending a lot of us to private prisons. They sent Freak to Mason, Tennessee.

I was back by myself. Freak was my real dog and still is to this day. I have a few years now under my belt and some good men I was dealing with as well. Out of nowhere, guess who shows up in the yard? My codefendant. Not to talk down on him but he never asked about me or sent me anything, not even a letter. There wasn't any love lost at all; it was all love. I made sure he was good and gave him the same game I gave Frank. It would have been all right anyway because he was a likable dude. Shortly more homies started to come to Lorton, The Hill. I gave them the same love as everyone else. Time is not easy, but you gotta make the best out of it. That is why I was doing my teaching and leading. Everything I write is a fact. Starting to get short.

One day, I went to classification for a review. They granted me to be transferred to another facility, and I really did not want to leave, but I did. Two years later, I was granted parole. Never will I forget my release date—August 17, 1996. My birthday was the next day. I was twenty-four years old at the time, from seventeen to twenty-four. That was my first adult experience.

Everything was new to me. I was like a newborn baby with limited help. I did not have anything. So much has changed when I got out. Some peers I knew were using hard drugs. The dudes I grew up with were not the same anymore. I could see it in their face and eyes. Women who were nice-looking when they were young now looked bad, the men as well. Remember I was only twenty-four years old at the time. For seven years, I was coming back to the same place that sent me to jail in the first place. Just like so many others, my first month was rough. At the time, my mother had a one-bedroom apartment. My grandmother had a two-bedroom apartment, with one of my uncles she was caring for. I was somewhat homeless. My family did not give a damn about me and looked at me as the black sheep of the family. When they needed something, I was always the first they called. It was tough adjusting, but I made it. I have always been a go-getter, so the challenge was nothing. Everything that I learned early on prepared me for this moment.

CHAPTER 3

I did not know coming home was going to be a struggle like this. Being away for so long affected my family in a major way. I was not worried about so-called fake friends doing anything for me. I understood that friendship was a juvenile time. My family really needed me. I was talking about the ones that were there for me. Just because we are blood, it does not mean anything to me. A family will cross you faster than a stranger. That is just how I feel. My brother was not the same when we were growing up together. He let life get the best of him. He was only twenty-two years old at the time with two children. A couple more years later he had another son. All he would do was drink and get high every day. It was like he did not have any drive to do anything but get high. From the gate, I was not feeling this. Life was still going on after I was gone. I never thought it would turn out like this.

One of my options was to stay with my mother in a one-bedroom apartment with her boyfriend at the time and my brother. I slept on the couch at the time. And his children would come over for the weekends. Where was I going to sleep? As a man, I could not be in this situation. Never did my mother deny me to stay there. She had her soon-to-be husband there, and she was happy. My other option was to stay with my grandmother. It was the same situation. She had a two-bedroom apartment with two men living with her—one was my uncle she had to care for because he was mentally challenged, and the other he was sleeping on her couch. He saw nothing wrong with that, and that was crazy. To top that off, she was still working her night shift job—an elderly woman leaving every night for work while my uncle slept all day, got high, and drank all night. I could not believe it. I came home to this. The only thing that came to mind was what I did best. I started hitting the block hard. At the time, that was my only option. It was not about being free. I had to act fast.

Being out of the house at an early age paid off for me. I ran into peers I knew growing up, and they were glad to see I made it home after all the years of being away. Being a street dude, which they already knew, asked the question, "What do you plan on doing?" I already knew what they were getting at basically and told them shit was fucked up. Whatever they had on them, they gave it to me. They gave me their numbers so we could hook up at a later time. So much was going on at the time in '96.

The ones who were once cool were no longer at all. If I were not the person I was, I would have been killed a long time ago. A lot of dudes were on some bullshit for real. Basically, if we were caught slipping, you were food to eat. I have been in the streets my whole life. I can honestly say they gave me the benefit of just coming home. Today, I respected that as well, and we had history before the bullshit. Growing up, I used to chill in other neighborhoods and was locked up with many peers. Respect was always there. Even now, the respect is still there. You are who you are. I had two neighborhoods where I could get started getting myself back, back around the same hood where I caught my first adult case. I would go around my mother's neighborhood late at night and have peers I knew there. My main goal was to get myself together and start helping my family out. Everything in life is about numbers. I had to get my numbers right. Again, math was my favorite subject in school, to turn nothing into something. What I was doing was serious because I had a purpose. Every day, I was up early, hitting the block. It was not easy either. Being gone for so long, the users did not remember me. They thought I was an undercover cop. The ones that did remember me told me why they felt that way. Clean-cut dude, well-groomed, and dressed nice—it made a lot of sense then.

The women who did not know me wanted to know who I was. My female homies I grew up with would tell me who was asking about me. It was like I was stepping on dudes toes around the hood.

My main concern was my paper. Truth be told, I was only around there because my grandmother was still living around there. People were always in my ear about getting caught up around there. Being incarcerated at an early age, you build relationships with others and have good jail buddies all over the city who are doing them and showing more love than the ones I grew up with.

I was not one to talk about people. I dealt with a person for who they were. I did not care about the materialistic things they had. I was always doing me regardless. To this day, I have a lot of love from men and women for who I am. Homies around my hood were not the same dudes. I started to see that firsthand. I had a few issues. It was not the time to get a life without parole. They say you forgive but never forget. There were a few months of beating both blocks up. I could see the fruits of my labor. I went from hand to hand to selling weight. I wasn't a kingpin, but I was good. you could feel my presence was at all the events with all the so called move shakers. I never looked up to another man. Do not get me wrong, I respect every self-made man. Nobody really gave me anything. I made my own lane. Anybody that really knows would say the same. That is why it was so easy for me to progress every time I came back home. I have been a go-getter my whole life. Even when I am incarcerated, if a dollar is there to be made, I am on it. Envy, hate, and jealousy are signs of weakness. I've never been a hater. Anyone should be happy if somebody comes up. It is not always the case if you are not a hater; you know I am not lying. Anytime a woman lets you know your peers are hating on you, that's really a problem. I am the same dude from the dirt; motherfuckers will hate you for anything.

C H A P T E R   4

Now the tables are turning in my favor. I started really looking out for my mother and grandmother every chance I got. I spoiled both of them with items they did not even know the designers' names. I enjoyed the smiles on their faces when we were together. Everything a dude was doing for their woman, I was doing it for them. Every upscale restaurant in and out of the city, they were there. I made appointments at hair galleries so their hair would look nice. Both had beautiful hair anyway. My family looks like we are Spanish. My grandmother was an American Indian.

Every time we went out, women were always flirting with me. Women respected me spending time with my mother and grandmother. The women I dealt with loved me even more for the love I had for them. I was not doing it to get points, that's just me. They were my heart, and I let them know I appreciated everything they did for me. I always had someone to look out for me. Everything you put out, you get it back good or bad in return. It is a true saying for real. I always had a support system. God always sent someone to bless me when I was down. My heart is pure anyway. I do not have a motive behind anything I did or do for a person. I don't need material things to justify who I am either. I always knew who I was at an early age. I was born a leader by nature. I heard this phrase so many times: "Dog, you always playing big." What is playing big? To me, it was normal shit. Playing big is temporary. I have been doing the same shit for years. You are who you are. I cannot fall off because without me, it is nothing. I told my good friend of mine that all the time. You will meet him as well later in this book.

Some things are just natural. Once I was out, I stayed in contact with my codefendant as well as other homies. I made sure a few good men were good also. Mind you, these are the same dudes who were out and did nothing for me or forgot where I came from. When a person leaves prison, they try to put that behind them. On the other hand, I'm with the struggle. Inside, behind the walls, or on the streets, never forget where I come from. During my first two months out, I made sure everybody was good. Not only was I giving whatever to the person they wanted me to meet, but I was coming myself. It was unbelievable coming back to a place where individuals were never coming back home. I made it out there and came back. Some would say I was crazy. The fact was, I know the feeling of somebody leaving you for dead. People on the streets keep money that somebody gave them. Family and so-called friends are lying to you at will.

I have been around good fathers and men in general, sending money out to the mothers of their children just to see them. We were not even an hour away. What type of shit is that? I know the feeling of getting dressed for a visit that never comes. That is a fucked-up feeling. Whoever can feel my pain knows I am not lying. I made it my business to do it myself. Never did I question myself about my actions in my life. Not only was I coming to see them, but also on trips, I would send them pictures—even just in the city, doing things like going to the clubs. I did that for the homies and other good men. It is the small things that count. I was not doing it to rub it in their faces. I am with the struggle, period. This went on for three years straight until it stopped three years later.

Now that I have been out for a minute, it was like I came home to this, meaning it was a lot of fake shit going on. People would tell you they loved you when it was time to depart. All the time was plotting on you for a minute for small shit. Women were around to get high or drunk at your expense. Everything was watered down. Many were just content with doing the same shit. Even right now, I can call on the streets, and the same shit is going on. In my mind, I am like, *This can't be life*. That is why I stayed on the move doing something. I got places to go and people to see.

There were times I just got in my car and just drove on Interstate 95. Most times, I would stop to see my family in the country. It was like the neighborhood ice cream truck pulling up when they saw me, and they knew it was going to be a trap star night or weekend. They were funny as hell. What they wanted to do was drink cheap beer and smoke cigarettes all day. Women did the same thing. Me being me made sure they were good. The funny part was that they were older than me. I was the big cuss to them. My lifestyle was too fast for them. At the end of the day, we were family. Part of the neighborhood was related to me somehow in some way. It was all love for me and a piece of mind at the same time. I had this one cousin who thought he was the shit down there. I would get with him later that night at times, depending on how I was feeling. There were times I would ride to Richmond, Virginia, with him. They had a club called Secrets. It was supposed to be an upscale club in Richmond. He loved being with me because he knew it was going to be a good night. We always bought a few bottles and got a booth. I was going to be leaving with something for sure. It was all love. As long as he was having a good time, I was cool with that. He was not doing that on a regular basis anyway. I was just chilling. That was my stress reliever when I went down there. Once the money in my pocket got low, I was a ghost. As long as they had a good time, I was cool with that.

I always spent some time with my great-great-aunt who raised me as well. That is the aunt I was with when my mom dropped me off. Her husband passed away in 1989, right before I got locked up. He was always happy to see me. He was there for me as well when I was incarcerated. Like I said before, never forget where you come from. She was spoiled as well. The little things made her day. Talking to her was enough for real. She was up in age at her time. That was my baby. I made sure she was put to rest well. She passed in 2004. She was a strong Black woman who loved people. She was always there for others. I will never forget that woman. She was like a mother to me.

My brother and I never really got along for many years. I feel like I played a part in his hardship in life. He lost his big brother to the system at an early age. I was seventeen, and he was fourteen years old when I left him. The bond was no longer there. Believe me, I tried my best to reach out to my brother. We just do not see eye to eye. He had a lot of jealousy toward me for what I did not know. His drug addiction has gotten worse. All I can do is pray for him. How can you help someone who does not want help? Everyone's walks of life are different. That is why I do not take anything for granted. Treat people the way you want to be treated. Carry the same principles on the street or in jail. I did not have to get locked up to know values.

It was always two things anybody could get from me—food and good drinks. Growing up my grandmother always cooked extra food just because anybody could always get a plate from her. That is the type of person she was. My mother is the same way. My values never changed with me. To this day, many different people would say the same thing, "Man, you always make sure we eat well." My best friend heard this so many times, and all he could do was laugh because he knew it was true. I showed the same love in the streets.

"You do not have it, fuck it"—that was my attitude. I am not going to give my last away unless you are worth it. You cannot fake it for so long. Time tells everything. I have been the same from the dirt. Not too many can tell me shit about life. With me, actions speak louder than words. Anything can come out of your mouth. Tupac was and still is my favorite rapper. Everybody who knows me knows that he said, "It took four years and a case to feel him, now they felt him."

Basically, he was saying he was the same person before all that. There are levels to everything. He died before his time as well. It was not just about selling records with him. The man was deeper than rap. If you are real, you know I am telling the truth.

CHAPTER 5

Loyalty and friendships mean a great deal to me. Now it is time to introduce a great friend of mine; he is the meaning of a true friend. We call him Joe, but actually, his name is Shelton. I really don't know where to start. That's how long he has been around. A dude from the hood who knew everybody. And his brother never had to be out there, which was a good thing. Whatever fashion was out, Joe had it as well. You would think he was selling drugs like everybody else. The hood knew better anyway. He would always be smiling all the time and loved to gamble. Every time I saw him, he was always fresh. He had a lazy walk about himself, so I started calling him lazy Joe. I was always in and out of jail all the time. My brother and Joe had a lot of history together as well. We used to be together with a few other childhood friends. The friendship they have today is another story.

Now that I have been in Lorton for about three years with my codefendant, a homie had just got there. He was a good friend of Joe and my codefendant. I knew of him but not really. He stayed locked up so much, and he was younger than me anyway. He started coming to see us both. He would come with my brother from 1992 until now—that is how long we have been together. Wrong or right, he was always there for me, not because of what I could give him but just genuine love for me. I got love for him like a real brother. His family is like mine. Everyone who knows us can tell you that he is one of the reasons I am writing this book. He always would say, "Man, you need to write a book about your life." Everything I do, he knows the purpose behind it. He witnessed everything I am writing about, except my much younger years.

When I am up, he is there. Nobody can tell him anything about me. He has been there the whole time. For twenty-eight years and counting, we've been together and for one another. Is that true friendship and loyalty? My story is no different from others. It is about real-life shit. I can't lie about the truth. You can tell if someone is lying. I cannot believe I am still here telling my story. So many childhood friends' lives were taken at an early age. The rest have a lot of time or life in prison. I just want people to understand how it can end for you. A boy to a man. I will always be for the struggle because that is who I am. It is not about fame or padding myself on the back., but it is about sharing awareness with the deaf, dumb, and blind. Everybody says they are real, but are they? I saw damn near everything when I turned forty-nine years old in August. You can't tell me much about the struggle. From seventeen to forty-nine, I have been on the streets for nine years, not counting the juvenile system. That is what I meant—a boy to a man.

I grew up in jail. Not everyone is willing to sacrifice their freedom for nothing in the world. Dudes will put their own mother under the bus to remain free. To get deeper into that subject also, this chapter is about loyalty and friendship. The circle is very small when it comes to friends. Real shit, my closest friends are mostly from jail. You do not have to grow up with someone to build a brotherly bond. All over my city, people know me not because of the street thing either. Good dude will stand for something that is why you gotta pick your friends wisely. Everybody is not your friend. Even your so-called soulmate would let you down. Tell everything that is why I move the way I do. Some do not care for me because I know the truth. It hurts and cuts deep. I can't keep faking it to make it. That is why I have love for my man Joe. You do not have to be somebody you are not. I want to be loved when I leave this earth, not hated. I have another female good friend like Joe.

Her name is Mona. She is a strong woman. This really was my soul mate. Again, loyalty and friendship. Being out a few months now, I ran across a girl I went to school with. I always used to chase her in the hallways during changing classes. Never will I forget this woman. When I did not have anything, she was there for me. I guess she saw something in me. She was also from the hood, so she knew the struggles of her brothers in the ghetto. It was the time I was getting on my feet. Also, I opened my eyes to things outside the hood. She was my rider-or-die chick, always a woman at all times but would ride for her man. Everything I was going through, she understood my situation, and she knew about my living conditions. I had to do what I could for my family. I wanted to give them a better outlet. I felt I owed them that much. My mother and grandmother were there for me my whole life. Never did they deny me anything.

About seven months later, Mona and I moved in together. It was the first time I ever lived with a woman. It was good for a while. Deep down inside, I was not ready for a relationship. This was all new to me. I was only home for nine months at the time. She was not trying to lock me down. Mona is the type any dude would love to be around. She is a real woman for real. She got your back if she fucked with you. Also, she knew about the women before her. They were just flings to me. All of them wanted that number one spot. I would never put them before her. I was just not ready for a relationship. One day, I decided to leave her. I bought a huge card and wrote a brief letter to her, letting her know why I was leaving. It was a cowardly move on me. I thought that was the right thing to do at the time. I damn sure was not going to be playing any games with her. That was my baby, and I respected her.

We parted ways, but we really loved one another. Today, we are still good friends, and I still love her dearly. It has been twenty-five years now and counting. To this day, we still talk and are there for each other. She moved on and had three children and is now doing great. She has a degree and properties, and her career is really going well for her. That should have been my soul mate. She will always be my baby. She feels the same way toward me. That is true love and friendship. I am the same dude who used to chase her in the hallways of school. I was saying that to say I never changed.

CHAPTER 6

Now that I and Mona had moved on, I had to find a spot to lay my head. I wasn't going to be living with women. I saw the issues dudes were going with that. My shit wasn't going to be in bags on the curb. Calling the police on me because you are in your feelings. I could never understand why a dude would pay another person's bills and maintain a household but got to put up with so much bullshit when you can just have your own and do you. I was not going to be a victim to that. So I started looking around for something. I had a buddy I used to visit in another section of the city. It was in Northwest, Washington, DC, where Howard University is. Anyway, I found a spot for the time being. Nobody knew where I was staying, which was a good thing. The buddy I used to chill with was really doing him at the time. He was always in my ear about coming on that side of town so I could fuck with him. I was cool with what I was doing. One day, we were together, and we went to his spot. He trusted me, and that's the only way I was there. He showed me a nice piece of money. He said this was just for today. He told me I needed to step up my game, and he was willing to show me how. Mind you, this is a dude I met in Lorton. We slept in the same dorm together. We became really cool. The dudes I grew up with were not even showing that much love. Again, he wanted me just on another level. He was dealing with dog food.

Anybody who knows about the game knows it's another level with that. That is a grown-man game for real. If you're serious about your paper, you will see results fast. Step by step, he showed me what to do. He even was selling it for me. He just gave me my money.

How many people are going to do that? He gave me the game for free and was helping me get it right. I still was doing my other stuff too. He did that for me for about a month. He already had a clientele and had been doing this for years. This was his thing growing up. Once you are known for something, that is how people will always remember you even if you change.

He was a born go-getter like myself. Every time I made it back home, it was always the same thing. "Dog, I know you're about to get you some money." Never, I got a job for you. He gave me good advice about bettering myself. It was the same thing. I would ask myself, "When you are gonna get some money?" The same people that you left behind they were in the way are the same people you come back to, still in the way. This new lane I was in was not a joke. People took this shit seriously. It was all about getting high for some. It was medication just to be able to function in the morning, just like that cup of coffee or cigarette first thing in the morning. Anybody that has experienced, any of them, knows I am telling the truth.

Now that the game was given to me. I started doing me. Once you know the game, you can move around anywhere it is sold. As long as you got something good and official, it is an open market. Like I said, this is a grown-man game. Somebody's always trying to run a game for whatever reason. One thing about being in life, whatever you're doing, somebody is going to be talking about you. From using to selling, believe that. All I heard was, "I heard you up town making money, heard you got something good." You got me, man. I am fucked up.

Everywhere you go, it's the same shit. My buddy and I became really close. When we're together, they really thought we were holding. That's what he is known for, and so am I. Everybody was begging from everywhere. The shit was funny. The same dudes that were so-called up in jail were on their heads in the streets. I could never understand some things at first. Like, a dude can be a neat freak in jail but a bum on the streets and can work like shit in jail but never get a job in the streets. That is some crazy shit. The same as so-called going hard on the streets, getting locked up, you might be fucking. From being somebody on the street to cleaning someone's cell for two fish, everything I speak about is real shit. There are no cut cards when you hear it from me. Real nigger shit, feel me. Of course, nothing lasts forever.

Now back to that three-year run, I got locked up in 1999 for a bullshit charge. Since I was on parole, I had to see the parole board. Before that, I beat the charge of an illegal search and seizure. I paid Bernard Grimm and Douglas Wood, one of the best drug lawyers at the time, to get me off. If you are from DC, again you know I am telling the truth. So back to Lorton I went, which was closing at the time. I saw the parole board, and those bitches gave me a five-year hit for a charge that I beat. The thing was, just because I beat the charge, I caught a new case, which was new criminal conduct. Also, my parole officer was a bitch.

I was not coming back to jail for dirty urine or some misdemeanor shit; I am not that type of dude. They knew this that is why they took my street time back and added two more years. I took it on the chin and was not looking to be punished like that. Again, my man Joe was right by my side as always. He made sure I was good along with some other people. Like I said before, I always had a support system. Joe would always make sure my mom was good, meaning checking on her to see if she needed anything and bringing her to see me. He always made that ride to see me here and there. I wasn't trippin off visits as long as I had some money and was able to make some more money, so I was good. That was just my way of doing time.

I made it back home in 2003. I was under the old law, so I got a few months off work. Back to where it counts, some say it starts in jail. I disagree that you can fake preparing yourself to be ready for society, but the temptation is there waiting for you. Basically, that man within yourself will come alive if you let it. You are who you are until you prove different, even to myself. I was in the halfway house now. The circle I was dealing with was coming at will, male and female.

Once I was able to get my passes, it was time to handle my business, pay off any fines, and get my licenses back. I was also going to get my food stamp card. It was free, so why not? Real nigger shit.

If you've been down this road before, you know it's real. You have to focus when you get back out there. I knew what it takes, so it was normal for me. Never was I nervous about returning back home. Again, this is the time when everything counts. I always found a job within the first two weeks after getting out. I told you I am always on my shit. If you have been to a halfway house before, you know it. The faster you start working, the faster you can get your weekend passes, and they want that money from you. See how I am always keeping it real by walking you through everything. This is for all the fake motherfuckers that kissed ass to get out.

All the dudes were cleaning up and taking their job so seriously. They got all the plans when they get out and can't even make it sixty days out. Start using drugs there. Never get a job or just leave. That's the pressure I was talking about. What was the purpose of doing all that faking for? It's the structure they are used to, having somebody always telling them what to do. When you get out, it separates the men from the boys—a boy to a man.

Now that I am out of the halfway house, it is time to find my way. My man Joe had bought me enough clothes to change for a week straight. Also, I had two pairs of boots and two coats. It was wintertime when I came home. Also, I was working on buying stuff here and there. I have only been out for four months now. This time around, my mom and her husband were homeowners. They had a three-bedroom home. I came home with less stress. They had a huge yard that I loved. I used to get up early and just meditate. She wanted me to take my time and feel my way.

One thing about being a parent is that they know their child. Her husband used to be in the streets as well. He never told me, but I knew. My mother was green to the fact. He changed his life around and gave it to God. She met him in the church she attended. He really is a real dude, and he makes my mother happy. I really respected him because he looked at my grandmother like his own. His mother passed away. If grandma loved you, you were all good with me. We had a man-to-man talk for the first time when I got home. That is why shit was fucked up for them. He was not living that life anymore. My mom believed in him, and it paid off. I still have respect for him to this day. As a man, I could not stay there. My mother's husband already knew I was not going to be there long. He was aware of me doing me.

Not long, I am back at it again. My man who gave me the game with the dog food was still doing him. I got tired of him coming to get me and making sure I was good. I am not that type of dude. Joe also knew it was a matter of time. He had been around me too long.

Really, all I had to do was fuck with my man, pass out the work, and get the money from the workers. Just like doing things my way, that is just me. Anyway, I got a spot within walking distance where we were doing us. I could bag up the work there or just chill if the block got hot. Never did we do business there. I called it the spot. Every time I went in, things changed a little, and I noticed customers were looking for work at night as well. That was even better for me. I was really hugging it. I had a spot two blocks away if I needed to get what I needed at any time. The only one who was aware was Joe. Not only was I selling dog food, but I had hard as well. "One-stop shop, bruh." The customers loved me. I was out there in the morning, then at night. Two months and I was back. When you are hungry and focused, there is no limit; it is up to you.

I always respected my mother's home. I was not coming in at all times of the night. Most times, I would tell women to pick me up. I did not stay out there all night. I closed up shop about 10:00 pm. My man was up, so he would always be on the move. He bought me a whip, and I really was saving my money. I made sure my mom was good. I would leave an envelope of $500 every two weeks. At first, I was giving her $200 every week just because. That is when I first got out of the halfway house. I did not want her to be seeing too much. Her husband was on point. I was just changing my clothes, and I was out. I was never really there. I told Joe I was about to get a spot to lay my head. I wanted to know what he wanted to do. He knew I was beating the block up. Whatever he needed goes without saying. Shit always comes together for me. Joe was already living with another good homie. They were sharing the apartment together. He told Joe he was moving out to be with his child's mother. Mind you, these were good working dudes. They were not in the streets. Shit, he told me about it, and everything else was understood. I moved in and took care of everything. I told him not to worry about the bills. I wanted him to take a break from the bills. Now he had room to do him. He was good anyway because of me. That was my way of saying thanks for everything. I bought new furniture for the apartment and basically lay it out. I was back in position once again.

Here we go. Dog, I see you doing you. Didn't you just come home? I was trying to figure out my moves. I had been home for seven months now and four of those months in the halfway house. See where am I getting at? Streets are always watching. Everything was going well for me. I can say this time, coming home was less stressful. I made sure I covered my ass with my parole officer. I was not working but got a woman I was dealing with to make me enough pay stubs for a year. She was an accountant for some firm. She also did her dad's books. He had a home improvement business. She used his business for my employment. If it was necessary, all calls from his business phone would go to her. All about who you know, feel me. Once I moved with Joe, I called my parole officer so he could do his walk-through. The only thing I had to do was take a urine test every so often. As long as you handle your business, you do not have to worry about them being on your line. I did not get high, so I was always ready. Also, I drank a lot of water because of that dog food; it could get in your system. Stay with me now or you get to handle your business. I am not coming to jail for bullshit. I am always going to be about getting a dollar.

Since you've been reading the chapters, I never had a problem adapting back out there. My work ethic was serious too. I was not working just to pay the bills. Most think that is the right thing to do—to pay bills and always be in debt. I'd rather be my own boss and pay myself. That was the plan. Later I will talk about that as well. I guess you can say I was always a risk-taker. Everybody wants the benefits, but nobody likes the sacrifices. Real shit. That is why some never get what they want and scared to take a chance to better their conditions.

Everything I am about isn't selling poison. That was a way to get my feet under me. I am a giver by nature. How can you help someone when you are fucked up? Later I'm going to get into that as well. Why do people love you when you're down but hate you when you're up? When you start to understand what really your purpose on this earth is, that is when you must follow the gift that God gave you. By now, Lorton is closed. Everyone from DC is in the federal system. It did not matter what charge you had you were going. Everyone from DC does not have a federal case. A lot of people did not know that. We have federal court as well. The feds just took over the DOC (Department of Corrections). My codefendant is still locked up to this day. Hopefully, he will be getting out soon.

I was back at making sure he was good and a few more homies, some good men I was cool with also. I always stayed the same no matter what. I never forget where I came from. At this time, you could get money sent to your account through Western Union. It was just extra for using it. If someone said they were going to send you money, you would know thirty minutes or less. You could not lie if you sent it. I had one homie who had me sending money all over the place, one of the ones who did not do shit for me during my first bid. Again, I am just that type of dude. I do not hold on to shit. "You are who you are point blank."

Of course, people was trying to get my number. You hear more shit locked up then being free on the streets. That is real shit; somebody always knows somebody. The word always got out. Real nigger shit. One thing I can say about my codefendant is that he never asked me for anything. I just did it for him. He got the most from me over the years just because of that. I guess I am cut from a different cloth. Not half of the shit I have done for people in jail or on the street they would have done for me. I know that for a fact. I guess that is one of the reasons God had a plan for me. All I heard for years was, "Dog, you are a good dude. I fuck with dog. He's real."

The good die young or get life without parole. That is why I take shit seriously. Any moment can be your last breath. I was always grateful for my blessings. I must give to receive; that is law. I will try to stay humble and live my life. You cannot blame others for everything that is happening to you. You got to get off your ass and make something happen.

CHAPTER 8

When you think you have all the answers, God always lets you know he is in control. In 2004, it was an all-star weekend break in Los Angeles, and I was headed there alone, but a good friend wanted to go as well. So we made it there and were ready to do us. We had a suite downtown LA, blocks away from the Staple Center. Remember this is LA; you had to come right. We were running into a lot of the ball players at LAX. It is a normal thing if you live out there. I could not believe all the money and some of these dudes dressing the way they were. You forgot when you have money that you can do what you damn please. Charles Barkley was staying where I was. Terrell Owens was there as well. He was on some different shit. Barkley was cool as shit. Anyway, we got settled in and started our day. We had some women there I was hitting. I did not want them to bump heads together. We were out of town and did not have time for the drama. We were trying to trick good. Anyway, fuck them. Like I said, I am in LA at all-star weekend.

The first spot we went to was Roscoe's Chicken and Waffles. We knew everybody from out of town was going to be there. That is just like any other place if you are coming to visit. Whatever known place you are in the building, you know tricking was at an all-time high. Women from all over were out there to get that paper. I got to respect the hustle. I went to Snoop Dogg's after-party and Allen Iverson's party. Damn, nearly every major hotel had a happy party with someone, I can't say it was all love. It was too late to get tickets for the game, but guess what? I made it happen. Big Boi from OutKast was doing the halftime show, and one of his men had VIP passes for courtside access. Being a street dude, I thought he was on some bullshit. He got us past security, and he escorted us courtside. That was big of him. We are courtside at the all-star game in LA, how big is that? We ran across the passes on a humble. Real shit can't explain the fun we had. If you are on some big boy shit, you already know how that weekend turned out.

I got back home to get some bad news. My great-great-aunt who raised me passed away. I was really hurt about that. Again, she helped raise me, and I felt the pain right now. That was my grandmother's only aunt left on her mother's and father's sides, so you can imagine how she pulled us together as a family. I already knew how I felt about both of them. I made sure she was put to rest well. I had joy and pain that week. Not long after, my grandmother got ill just out of the blue. She never was sick, not to my knowledge anyway. I found out her liver was going bad on her. She was always weak. She stayed in and out of the hospital. I made sure I was there for my baby. Whatever she needed or wanted, she had it. They wanted her to be in a rehab center. Never would that happen on my watch and my mother's either. So my mother retired early from the DC public school system to take care of her mother. She had a caretaker as well. She was getting weaker and weaker, but she was always a fighter.

On her good days, she, my mother, and I would go out to eat. Women love to eat out. She is from the South and loved her pork. Her favorite was ribs. Some were so tender that the meat would fall off the bone. At the time, Houston's was still open. It was a restaurant that sold good soul food, an upscale restaurant in Georgetown, near Georgetown University. If you do not know the area, anyone who has been to Houston knows about their food. She enjoyed the ribs there. Whatever would put a smile on her face, I was for it. Every time is on hold when I am with them. That is real talk at this time. I was home only a year, but it felt longer. It was moving so fast like I never was gone. It is always like that when I am home.

One day, I was walking up the block. It was jump-out day, so everything was closed down for right now. I was walking and a customer ran up to me, asking where my workers were. I told them the people were out there. So I walked from her and a jump-out ran up to me. They must have been watching her from a car or truck somewhere. I couldn't tell you which. They must have thought I gave her something, which I did not. I already knew it was jump-out day. Also, I had people to take care of stuff like that. They put cuffs on me and started searching the building. A lot of people kept their work in the building's hallways. They so-called found three bags of dog food. I was like, "Really, three bags?" Come on, man, I never went in my pockets. They tucked me up anyway. I went to jail, and the judge gave me a five-day hold because I was still on paper. My five-day hold was up, and they gave me PR. That right there was my warning to my pole officer about the arrest. He knew that bullshit charge was going to get dismissed at my next court date. I faxed my parole officer regarding the bullshit charge. He never said any more about it. I thought he was waiting for the outcome of the case. I kept doing me as usual. I had a funny feeling about my parole officer. When we were getting the funeral together for my aunt, my cousin asked me if I could get him something. I am all about a dollar, so I told him, "Let me take care of this first." When everything was over, he came up by himself. I made sure he was good. About every two weeks, he would come back up. He was like, "Because you need to come down here," so I went down there the next day. It was less than an hour. Same please before in the early chapters. I knew everybody anyway, so it was all good. I started going down when they needed me, or they would meet me halfway at Potomac Mills. Shit was going good, extra money for me.

One time, I went down in a rental car because my buddy and I were going out of town to take care of something. A local cop got behind me and pulled me over. Everything was legit. I had my license and the rental car agreement papers. He said I was speeding. I ran my license through. Guess what? He had a damn warrant on me. I am like, "You sure? Can't be." He ran it again. He said, "Son, we have a federal warrant on you."

Remember, I am in the country. That is big to them. The damn parole officer put a warrant on me for that bullshit charge I caught. I thought that my buddy had a license, but he did not. The car was in my name as well. They were not tripping off him. They just wanted me. They asked me if there was anything in the car as if I was going to say yeah. They took the car. A traffic stop turned into 156 months of federal time; all this happened in one year of being out. God was warning me all the time.

CHAPTER 9

After everything I've been through, does that make me the bad guy? Now that I was back in the system. I was really depressed but not to the point that I would hurt myself. It was just the thought of me leaving and being back in less than two years. I came back after 5 years. I got up to 300 pounds just eating for the first two years. And once I got over it, I was good. It was just a phase I was going through. I was not going to beat myself up about it. I got to do time and not let it do me. Once people know you have a lot of time, they are gone in the wind. I was not new to what would happen. I already knew who was going to be there, the same support system for years. They were hurt but understood me. I thought anyway. Sometimes people just want you there, especially the ones who really love you for you. I did not understand that at first. Love does not pay the bills. What are you going to do if an emergency comes up and nobody aids and assists? That is a fucked-up situation to be in.

My mother would always say, "I am going to pray on it." God will answer your prayers if you are sincere. A good friend told me you cannot save everybody. That was not the case at all. She said, "And what were they doing before you came into the picture?" It made a lot of sense to me. I was not going to hear that if it was someone I cared for or was there for me. That was just how I felt.

I had been in for about five years now down in Jesup, Georgia. This was my second facility. I couldn't stay in one spot for a long period of time, either leaving on a disciplinary transfer or when my points dropped. Another way, if you are *L*, you're right. I called home one day out of the blue, and my mother did not sound like herself when the call went through. She said, "Son, got something to tell you. Your grandmother passed today."

I could not even talk anymore. That was the lowest I ever felt. The last time I saw her was in 2004. That was the only regret I had—not being there to see my grandmother off. The only person I could talk to at the time was my man Joe. It hurt to recall that moment. Anybody who has lost their mother or grandmother can relate. I'm telling you now, I do not care how strong you think you are; I cried like a baby. As we know, time heals everything. Now, I am working on trying to give some of this time back.

The crack law just passed. If you had a crack cocaine charge, you know what I am talking about—an 18–1 ratio to powder cocaine. At first, it was 100–1. See how they made examples of Black men in America—same drugs, just with baking soda added. Again, you're going to hear all the truth from me. I was trying to get as much time off as possible—not just me, but whoever had a cracked case. They had dues locked up all over the system since 1986. That was when Reagan was in office. It was a war on drugs was what they called it. Putting you on the game, that was for the ones that did not know that. Do me a favor and read the new Jim Crow if you have not read it yet.

My time was reduced, so I was close to home in Cumberland, Maryland, an FCI facility. I got three years off. When I got to Cumberland, it was short, meaning two years or less, which was considered short. My mandatory minimum was ten years for possession with intent to distribute cocaine / possession of a firearm / furtherance of drug trafficking crime. That was a mandatory 10 years alone, and I could not get around that.

Being in Cumberland really opened my eyes. The shit I was seeing was crazy to me. A lot of young dudes were coming in fucked up. Older homies to me were already washed up, coming off the streets. I am talking about somebody nineteen to twenty-one years old. Every story was about drugs. I had more stories and pictures to show them, and I've been in for going on ten years. I was glad to be close to home, but I wasn't at the same time.

I could not believe nobody wanted any money. Everything was about K-2, booting up, or heroin—basically, any type of drug. I like talking to my young homies because that is where I am from. DC did not look down on them either. I just could not believe what I was seeing and hearing. Babies on hard drugs already. That was the new wave, and they were really gone. I did not see anything wrong with what they were doing. I was here at the door, just doing me until they called my number. All that planning—I did not have to do that. I already knew what to do, handle my business like a man. Everything counts out there to me.

I was talking to a homie about the streets, trying to pick him about what was going on out there, really bidding for real. I had been seeing so many coming from jail now. He was twenty-six to twenty-eight years old, back on violation, and looked like for dirty urine. I could tell his kind. I'd been doing this shit too, LOL. Anyway, he said, "OT, you about to go home, right?" That is something I had to get used to as well. I said yeah. He told me to go out there and sell single cigarettes and was serious about it. This was 2013. I could not believe he said that. In my mind, I was like, "Is everybody a junkie out there?" I made him a bag so he could have something to eat and also wash his ass. I did it because he just got there. The bag was worth $40, and he was talking about buying a pack of cigarettes. That is when I knew where I was coming home to—a wake-up call

Getting real now, I have a halfway house date. They gave me four months of halfway house time. It was September 17, 2013, a week before my mother's birthday. January 9, 2014, was my date to get out of the halfway house. I was gone for a decade this time. So what would I be dealing with when I got out? My day came, and it felt good. Joe met me and drove me around for a minute before I went to the halfway house. He wanted me to try this new spot. It was called American Best Wings. He knew I loved wings. The halfway house was only three blocks away. What I was seeing was sad. My homie was right. Damn, nearly everybody was selling cigarettes and K2. I thought they were selling heroin the way the crowd was. This was at the gas station. All this was new to me, and I saw it firsthand myself.

I was going to stay with my mom again for the second time. They already came to the house for the walk-through, making sure it was livable and safe for me to be there. I did what I had to do to get my first pass. I went to see about my license and to get a printout of any ticket I may have. I wanted to take care of that ASAP. That was my first goal—getting my license and a job. One of my buddies hooked me up with a job. It was a part-time job, but I did not care. As long as I got my weekend passes, I was good. On my first pass, for a few hours the next Friday, I had my first weekend pass. It felt good to be lying in a real bed again. Mom was so happy I was back home, and shit, I was too, believe me. My brother was living there as well. He really let drugs get the best of him. I could not believe that it was my blood brother. That was how bad he was looking. I always got up early in the morning and went to sit at the kitchen table, and there was nothing but a bunch of past-due bills—talking about a lot. My brother slept in the basement, and when he came up to use the bathroom, he greeted me.

I said, "Bro, do you know about these bills?"

He said, "I don't touch Mom's bills."

To myself, I am like, really? How can you say that when you live here? I saw he did not care about shit. Being me, I waited until my mother got up, called her to the kitchen, and pointed to the bills. "How long has this been going on?"

"Do not worry about it. You have enough on your plate. You just came home, I got it."

I felt so bad; I could tell it had been going on for a while. My brother just looked stupid. This had been going on for years. She never told me about the household because she did not want me to worry. Going back to work, my friend said, "What were they doing before you got there?" not referring to my family, just in general.

What am I supposed to do as a man and son? Let it pass for right now. I had only been home a month now and was still in the halfway house the next week, and got my pass again. I went to the mailbox to get the mail and saw a Wells Fargo letter from the bank—another past-due bill. I came to find out my mother's home was in the final stages of foreclosure.

I could not believe it—she was backed up that much. Her husband was separated from her. This was real personal but real shit. What was I to do? I did not have any money like that to help out. The only person I could talk to about this was my man, Joe. He just listened to me. One thing he knew was that my mind was made up of nothing you could tell me. Also, he knew how real shit was at the time, just coming back in a situation like this one. What would you do?

While I was in the halfway house, I was talking to one of my old female friends. We were just talking about when we were together, and I could tell she never really got over me. She was in a relationship, but she was not happy. I could tell women are really desperate for a man, especially Black women. They are scared of being lonely. It is sad but true. Basically, I asked her for a loan. She knows I am not a bum-ass dude or a user. Also, we had a history together. Even before she got where she was in life, I was there for her, not bragging shit, just keeping it real.

"What do you need the money for?" She thought I was trying to buy some work with the money. Pretty much I was, but I was not going to tell her that. After about a week of me constantly asking her, she agreed and gave me $5,000. This woman is not the type to just give men money. Even her own family was not good for that kind of bread. She knew she was going to get her money back.

Cutting the chase, as soon as I completed the halfway house I bought myself some work and got a rental car—only four months of being out. I know I am a crash dummy, crazy whatever. Some would say that was her problem. Playing games on a woman for that $5,000 just to fuck up? My shit is really not that type of dude. That's what separates men from boys—you are who you are! I found out the hard way—motherfuckers do not want no money. Everybody wanted a favor or getting fronted. What type of shit is that? I got broke even the first time around but still had my job. My boss gave me the full eight hours. Now everything takes time; I know that. It was the same game, different players, that's all. I started to see what everybody really wanted and even told my brother what I was trying to do. I was jumping out there for a reason. This shit is not a game. He smokes PCP heavily. I noticed everybody wanted it. It is nothing I cannot sell. I had to get with the program. I would sell a whale of water if I had to. I wanted my brother to be my outlet at the end where he was hanging out. You already know what happened—he fucked the money up smoking the shit and letting the women get over on him. He was just a user; it was not in him. I had to get it how I lived, and before I knew it, everything was coming together. PCP moves like dog food. As long as you got something good and you are out there, you're good. Most smokers only like the late night, and another thing is they might do anything off that shit. I had to do what it took.

For a long time, the bills went down. To this day, she still has her home. She was in a better place once I came back home. She worked too hard to lose her home. Now it is time to focus on me. My friend said I could take my time and pay her back. I was not even out a whole year and paid her back with extra just because.

She had a mortification hearing with the bank to start a payment plan. She had to pay a certain amount every month for six months straight. I helped her with that—that was the most important bill of the household. I took care of all the other bills. That way, I knew it was done. Honestly, she did not want me in her business, which I respected. I had to take control of the situation. For six months, she met her obligations with the bank. Everything was back in order. Once I saw everything was back, I moved out. I could not be around my brother any longer. I found a place and got myself a car three months out of the halfway house. Some might say I could've done it another way, but I did not. That was my way, and I can't take back what is done.

CHAPTER 11

I was out for a year now, and it was my first birthday being out. I did not do much but had a nice time. I told myself that next year, I would really do me. I owed it to myself. I always planned on having my own business, but I always got incarcerated before I reached that goal. It took time to receive my food manager's license. You needed that to sell any food. Also, I could use this to manage any business as a manager as well. My goal was to buy a food truck. Cooking is my passion.

Years ago, I received my apprenticeship in culinary arts in Lorton. I really wanted this to come together. That is why I was taking the steps. I needed it very seriously. I did my homework about the truck. I even had a location to prep my food. The place was called Union Kitchen. Basically, it was a 24-hour kitchen, but you had to be a member. It was great for small businesses. Everything was there for you. You just had to bring the supplies with you. I did not have to lease a building for business, avoiding unnecessary expenses that one might not have at the time. It was very convenient. Also, it was a network place for other businesses to share. The only thing that was stopping me from starting my business was being on probation. You cannot have your own business on federal probation. Basically, you cannot work for yourself.

I was still on the streets but made sure I kept a job. I understood that was my lifeline, meaning you could get a loan from credit unions, cars, and whatever. It was up to you what you did with it when they gave you the money. I always had credit but not like I wanted it built up. Credit is everything; a higher score means lower interest rates. Anybody on their adult shit already knows what I am talking about. That's why I came out and did what I had to do. If I was out for years, there was no telling where I would be. I've always handled my business. People have been on the streets all their lives and haven't done half the shit I did. That's why I asked the question: What would you have done? I was never a dummy, there were just choices I needed in life. It cost me, but I would not take it back; it made me the man I am today—a boy to a man.

God always had a plan for me. Everything was on track for me. I love living by myself. Some would go crazy not waking up to someone, man or woman. I just loved to have the option to have company or not. When I did have company, they did not want to leave. I was the perfect catch for a woman—a single man with no children and had my own shit. This was a dream come true for many women. The odds of a woman to a man are ten to one being Black. I was considered the total package deal. This shit I am talking about has been going on for years with me. I was not just talking for the sake of talking. Real nigger shit every place was laid out. I knew how to cook, clean, and maintain a household. In my mind, what do I need a woman for? That is why to this day, women care for me. Never did I lie to them or run a game. I always did me. They respect me for that. It was up to them if they dealt with me. You are who you are. I could have it my way but not the type of dude. I guess that is why I was always blessed. You get back what you put out in life. "A boy to a man"

Now in my second year home for my birthday, I told myself I was going to really do me. I went to Hawaii by myself. I could not explain the experience I had. I did not want to come back. I couldn't tell you that. The feeling was, I was living my best life. People from all over the world visit Hawaii. The feeling was like a 400-pound dude saying, "Fuck it. I am jogging on the beach with my shirt off." Real shit, if you've ever been there, you know I am not lying. Couples come there to get married. They get married on the beach. That is where all the surfers come to serve from all over the world. It is truly a beautiful place. I've been to a lot of places, to be honest. For the past five years, I have gone somewhere four times, and I'll delve into that later in the book. Again, people in my business—dog, you're getting money. That is why it is level to everything you do. A person will take their last to buy the latest fashion but never invest in a trip. That trip cost me $2,500, not including what I spent. It's a once-a-year experience, not like it is every day.

The simple things are a lot to some. Anybody you respect or look up to should motivate you and want the best for you, but they don't. Once you find out the truth about them, you might look at them differently. As the saying goes, "Game is to be sold, not told." I have been talking my shit since when nobody was not listening until it happened to them, and now they understand. That's why there are levels in life; sometimes you need somebody to show you the big picture. Someone will respect you more if they know your story. It is basically saying that if he or she can do it, so can I. That is all I am about. There were brothers I know who never went back to prison. They must have a support system waiting for them. Everyone does not have that. I was one of them. I really respect them dudes to the utmost. They always used to say, "Dog, I respect you, man, you going to do what you got to do." They witnessed it themselves. I am all about the struggle and the people. You have to go through something to know where you are. Going in life, anything that is easy to me is not worth it. It is sad to me how the youth are lost so much. I do not blame them. Everything starts in your household. Some parents never prepare them for life challenges. I call it parenting of today.

They spoiled them to the point of making them bums at an early age. How do you not have support at eighteen years old, living on the streets, stealing out stores just to get high? When I was coming up, users did that. Now, people hustle, selling soap, toothpaste, and Tide Pods. Real shit, I am about truth. This is what I came home to. Again, I never fell victim to any of the above. That is why I keep saying I am blessed. Never will I get big-headed about anything. I have been living in a small bathroom, which is a cell, damn near all my life. I told my buddy Joe one day that I could sleep in a large closet, the one with two sides to them. It was a joke, but I was dead ass serious. All I needed was a blowup bed, and I'll be good. I am saying all this that if I can do it, anybody can. Do not think I am looking for someone to feel sorry for me. I just want the ones like myself to know that I feel your pain. My story is no different from so many others. If you never experienced it, I aim to give you a vision of someone like myself.

CHAPTER 12

Being out this time is the longest of my life. I had to deal with the times, which was easy for me. It was like a movie; I saw it over and over again. Like Scarface, that movie made everyone want to get some money. Now everything was watered down. I did not take much anymore. The simple things meant a lot to people now. It took me some time to understand that I couldn't lie even after being locked up. People had levels. In this day and time, morals and principles are no longer prevalent. Everybody forces themselves or seeks what they can get. Some will sell their soul just for a cheap drink. I saw this with my own eyes. I could have fallen victim if I was not strong. It was everywhere you went, like lost hope and purpose for people.

My circle is a positive group. It is very small. They would have been in my shit. I was not going to let myself down anyway. I was getting better job opportunities all the time. The doors would always open up for me. I did not mind working as well. I wasn't planning on working forever. Again, I have been locked up more than I have been on the streets. When I first came home, I went to Navy Federal Credit Union. I opened up a Roth account, basically a retirement plan, just like when you have a 401(k) plan. The money is taken from your check. I was paying myself with my own money.

As you've been on this journey with me, my working history is limited due to the choices I made at an early age in life. I always put money into that account for a rainy day. I started late, but believe me, I'm going to have a nice piece of change when I retire. I have always been a planner; most people do not know that about me. I have two life insurance policies on me, and both my mother and Joe are the beneficiaries. I also put one on my mother, and I am her beneficiary. They are the only two I trust for something like that. I have always been on my grown-man shit. I had to help bury my sister and uncle since I'd been out. I never had a policy, and I'm glad I was able and in the position to help.

You never know when God calls your number. My mother told me I grew up too fast. I never was a child. Everything was always natural to me. I always tried to plan my work and work the plan. I never had time to waste. My moves always counted. At the time, I had a job working with the mentally challenged. I really liked that job. My job title was to maintain the house—laundry, cooking, cleaning, and making sure they were ready in the morning for their programs. I had the graveyard shift. It was a house of four adults. They loved me for real. Sometimes, I had to work on the weekends. When I worked the weekends, they already knew it was on. The company had a van. Some staff just kept them in when they worked the weekends. It was just a job to them. For me, it was an adventure. I was doing me anyway, so I did not mind. We would be everywhere. All of them got checks monthly. So whatever they wanted, I got it for them. It was like I was with four grown children. They wanted everything they saw sometimes when it was nice outside. I would buy food for the grill and have a cookout for them. My mother had a huge yard. One of my uncles is mentally challenged. That's why I could relate. That was a wonderful experience I had with them. I got fired from that job. I guess you're saying how.

I had a coworker who worked before my shift. She would always say I dressed nicely. "You have a nice SUV truck, what's tripping off that shit?" It was a 2017 SUV; everybody's thirsty out there. Anyway, sometimes I would ask her to stay a few hours until I got there. I had some other runs to me. She did not have a life anyway. Everything is about a phone now, and that is people's life. That was all she did. Also, I would give her a few dollars for doing it.

Moving along, she told the owners of the business I was coming in drunk. She was a friend of one of the family members. They believed her, and they let me go. This was all over because she asked me for a few dollars to help her pay a bill.

I told her, "I do not be fucking you. Why are you asking me?"

She was really in her feelings at that time, and I was drinking that night. I can be a motherfucker at times. True story: now I am not working, but I am good.

I hung out and drank more. I was the life of the party. Honestly, I was just doing me—that is all. To me, I was taking a break for a minute. A job is nothing for me to get. Not too many people would get me a job if I really wanted one. I was like, "Fuck a job, really." For about six months, I did not work. I handled my business regardless. I got bills to pay, filmy. Every chance I got was in the air, going on vacation for a few days. Shit, I owed it to myself to do me.

One day, my man, Joe, said, "You need to get another job. All you do is drink every day." I would buy one or two half gallons of Grey Goose every day. Anybody who knows me will tell you I am not lying. I would drink Goose every day and party. That was when I knew what I was doing was not normal. A dude told me, "You spend $350 a week just drinking. That's $1,400 a month just on bottles." I was like, "Damn, I never looked at it like that." It was basic shit to me. Drinking every day costs me in the long run. I'll tell you about that later.

One day, Joe said, "I went online and put an application in for you. They should be calling you soon." I thought he was bull-shitting. He was dead ass serious. They called me, and I went to the interview. I got hired the same day. Is that a friend or what? We both worked at Georgetown MedStar Hospital. My job title was a food service worker. Basically, I delivered the food to the patients and took their orders. Mind you, people from all over the world came to Georgetown to get treatment. As time went on working there, all the staff members on the floors I worked on loved me, including the family members of the patients, doctors, and nursing staff, everyone.

I received three spirit awards. A spirit award is when you are nominated for the values of service, patience, first, integrity, and respect—a team player all around the board. They used to call me Uncle Charles. Joe used to come visit me all the time just to see what I was doing. He was there before I got there. He pretty much knew everyone in the department they worked at. Once they got to know me, it was over. They used to call him broke and try to charge him for everything. It was funny because he knew them before me. They were joking with him, but Joe did not like that shit. That's just the effect I have on people. I am a people person. I really enjoyed that job. It was just the hours. I had to work twelve-hour shift. You really did not have a life for real. Basically, I worked, slept, and did it all over again the next day, but it was cool.

Joe's birthday came up. He never really wanted to do shit for real. It was my man's birthday, and I was up. His cousin and I rented a restaurant/bar. We had the upstairs part. She took care of everything. I let her do her; I just gave her the money. I also got a suite at the hotel. It was an event going on in the ballroom. We were in the building like the rock boys. Everybody was showing him love. It was his birthday. We drank all day. I know I was anyway.

We stayed until the next morning. I noticed my chest was hurting. I mean really hurting. I thought I had heartburn. I would get it all the time, but it was not heartburn. I had a minor heart attack and did not know it. All this time, I thought it was gas. It was my body telling me to slow down. Remember I told you that God was giving me the signs all along. I let it pass. I kept drinking and smoking cigars. One day, I was over at my buddy's house, watching a basketball game, still drinking and smoking. The right side of my body went numb. My words were coming out with a slur. I was having a stroke. Never would I imagine that this would happen to me, but it did. Again, God warned me to slow down.

I was in the hospital for about a week. I did not have to go to rehab. I got my speech back a few days later. It could have been much worse. I was lucky. Of course, I had to get medically cleared before I returned back to work. I went back to work. Now I am on medications. The hours were getting too much for me to handle. I just resigned. I stopped drinking for a while but started back. Now I am drinking and smoking and taking medications. I was not even supposed to be doing that on meds.

I started stressing more about what I did not know. My main goal was to get off paper. That was my concern. Honestly, I was not myself. Looking at me, you would not have known I was depressed. Sometimes I would just start crying for no reason. I would mention to Joe about the medication I was taking. I started thinking too deeply like everybody was against me. I knew some were hating. I started looking at everybody differently. I guess I was just trippin'. I just kept doing me and handling my business. All I was telling myself was, "Damn, 'bout to get off paper." That is a dream everyone, like myself, wanted. Once you are off paper, you can do what you want. Do you want to smoke weed? You could. I did not have to worry about having dirty urine. I had a lot planned for this day. I'll get back about finishing probation.

There were two people who really witnessed my growth—Joe and my mother. I used to tell Joe, just joking, but I held it down for five summers. "What more you want from me?" Meaning, some come home, and the pressure hits them ninety days out. You can fall off quickly in the streets. It was a joke but the truth. Somebody's always praying for your downfall. You can smell it, taste it, and most importantly, feel it. When someone thinks you are outshining them, you can feel the hate. At the end of the day, what I do is about all love. Real talk, everything has changed. What people would be standing for is far gone. Nobody cares about anything anymore. That is just like the street code snitching. Snitching is at an all-time high. I can't keep up with it. Every day, someone turned sour. The ones who say they don't fuck with rats do—somehow, someway. They are everywhere—family members, enemies, even dudes you've been around every day, especially if it is beneficial to someone. When you start knowing the truth, you are a threat.

People who know the truth get killed. You are a hated man if you know the facts. It is crazy that a race always glorifies others. Every major drug lord is a rat, not a neighborhood dealer—that is small shit. The mob was filled rats, so where is this so-called street code? This was bigger than nickels and dimes. The United States government has rats all over the world. Who the hell are you? Do not get me wrong, I am not with that telling shit. I've always been a stand-up dude. I will always do my time, hands down. I cannot even speak for the ones who might read this book. It is real, y'all. I do not have time to be faking. Basically, nobody stands for nothing these days, male or female. Sometimes you gotta be aware of what you are saying. It makes sense first. That person has to deal with their actions. Only God can judge them. For the ones who still stand for something like myself, just keep it moving. We got too much other shit going on in this world to be focused on dumb shit.

CHAPTER 14

Another Black man will kill his own brother. They're not going to do anything to the ones who don't give a fuck about you. They would keep their foot on your neck and don't do anything. Y'all know who I am talking about. It's always the ones who will say what they will do but never do shit, just trying to put a battery in somebody's back to crash out. Women have more hearts than these dudes out here. A lot of people are living lives. Like Boosie's song titled "Wake Up," that is some real shit! I do not have all the answers but have awareness, period. I gotta practice what I preach. I always did, but I wanted to be positive about it now. I cannot be halfway in, halfway out. I have a purpose on this earth. God gave me a gift. I never used it properly. It's about reaching the ones you're able to reach. I cannot save everyone. If I reach someone, I do my part. That is why, it is about giving back and not taking all the time. Again, I am always a giver. It is always how I give that is the problem. I cannot tell someone to do something when I am not doing it. My life is about purpose now. I have been a self-made man, not tripping off daughters. I want to be a part of the solution, not the problem. I am for the movement. Talk is cheap. Everything is about action.

The brotherhood is already there. It's time for me to play my part. As you can see, I have a lot to share. Just like the saying, "Knowing is half the battle." That is why we must depart from people, places, and things. When you are trying to go somewhere in life, never forget where you came from. You still have to go where you are going because you might get sidetracked. The haters always get the high beams on you. You really find out who people are when you change. Most will congratulate you, and others will wait for your downfall. That is why I have always been about the struggle. You are who you are! What does not kill you makes you stronger. Some of us know. Some things are not healthy for us but still be a part of it. That is like smoking a pack of cigarettes. The back of the pack warns you. You can get lung cancer, but you still smoke them. That is called suicidal thinking. That is why I must change my life. I kept getting the same results, starting something, and never finishing it. I was spending more time in jail than in the streets. It just doesn't add up. Something has to give. That goes for all the ones like myself. You know who I am talking about—the ones who think just like me.

It has been a journey for me. I feel honored to share my story. All this is coming from the heart. I don't have to lie about anything. When you are telling the truth, you cannot do anything but feel it. I hope what I am saying can awaken that inner self. You have or once had. It is good for all of us. It took me years to get where I am now. I cannot complain at all. I had my fair share of experiences, good and bad. I have a lot of miles on me as well. That is just like Tupac; he has been dead damn nearly twenty-five years. You still can play his shit today and feel his pain, the message he was trying to give us. That means something to me—having something to say. I want to be loved, not hated. Now that I know my purpose, it is not an excuse. My mother will be a senior citizen this year. I cannot be locked up in anyone's system. She's been there for me my whole life. It is time for me to be there for her. I cannot live with myself with the thought of something happening to her and I am locked away. For me, that's not an option.

I lost a part of me already being in the system. I cannot lose another one being selfish. That is another thing. Whatever went on with your upbringing, your parents gave you the gift of life. I know they may have done some things that scarred you in life. We, as humans, are not perfect; we all make mistakes. So someone has to be the bigger or better person. If you are a God-fearing person, it tells you to honor your mother and father. You only get one mother and father. When they are gone, you are going to feel it, believe me. I thought about some times I used to see peers call their parents all types of names and disrespect them in front of whoever. To this day, a lot of them are reaping what they sow. Some are bums, sick from illness, or just fucked up. That's why, I stress so much about being blessed. Whatever choices I made in life, I treated everyone with respect. Never could I take advantage of someone because they had a sickness. The tables always turn. Now they are clean, doing better than the ones who were selling poison to them. True story.

The game was over, but I was not ready to let it go. My two buddies and I put together our money to purchase a large amount of work. If everything went right, we would be good. Dealing with ones in your own city is always bullshit. Also, they did not want you to get ahead. If you have good ties with out-of-town, that's your best bet. It takes money to make money. Anyway, it did not go well. The three of us felt that loss. You win some, and you lose some, not like this one. If you've been in this situation before, you know what I am talking about. We had to take it on the chin. We all have big boy bills. The bills have to be paid. We all had something to hold us over. The lost was a major one. So we are all trying to get some of our money back. True story.

I started really being back out there. You would not have known I was hurting just by looking. I was feeling it for real, especially every time another bill had to get paid. You know the feeling when you are trying to get back. Everything is on hold. Shit, I started taking risks I normally would not take. In my mind, it is what it is. I kept doing what I was doing, staying out later and later. We all know all days aren't the same. Also, this 2018 money was not the same anymore. It is hard to make a few dollars now. I have to put a lot of work in and get back a little in return. If you have some money, better hold onto it.

I started coming out of Virginia with one of my buddies. He was trying to get back as well. So we would be together doing us. This was where he was doing him. Again, if it's about a dollar, I am there. Everything was everything. He turned me on to some of his people. We are like family, so it's all love. The people I deal with have each other's back. It's not just about the street life. The people I was dealing with spit money. The only thing they might be anywhere but nearby. I would meet them and keep it moving. I was not hanging out in Virginia. I just came to take care of business. Everything was going smoothly.

One day, a customer told me he was in Arlington. He spent good money with me. I did not mind meeting him. He texted me the address where he was. We met, and he got what he wanted. Now when I was about to leave, his friend asked me if it was cool to get my number. The only reason I was here, was because of who called me. The person I came to meet said she was a good person. Someone getting high might say anything. I know this every time we deal with one another. He was never on no bullshit. Also, he spent good money with me. I gave her my number just because of her friends.

One day, she called. She gave me her location, and I met her. She got what she wanted and that was that. Two weeks later, she called me again, and the same thing happened, and I left. She wasn't calling me every day. I thought she was just working with other people, getting something on the side. One day, it was slow. So I was in the house chilling, and she called. It was getting near rush hour. I did not want to get caught in the evening traffic on the way back. I left so I could get right back. I made it there where we would meet. She texted me. She told me she would be there in five minutes. She never did that. It dawned on me, but I let it go.

Out of nowhere, plainclothes police were everywhere. It was the Arlington County task force. She set me up good. This was December 13, 2018. My probation was up on January 9, 2019. I had twenty-seven days left to be off paper. That was my goal to get off paper. Not being patient cost me again. I could not believe this was happening. I kept saying, "Fuck with this bitch." So they got me out of my truck. They were trying to run a game. They wanted me to basically rat myself out like I was green. That is what they used to do out there. Nothing really happened. Getting caught with drugs is the biggest thing to them. I could not eat for days. It kept rewinding what happened over and over again in my head.

Now I was thinking about my probation. Also, I was dealing with this new case. This was the commonwealth. Everything is about money. It was mandatory to get a paid lawyer. The feds put a warrant on me. I spent the next weeks sitting at the detention center. I had to see a judge after I finished with this new case. I could not believe I was back in again. Being back locked up really opened my eyes up. They had me under surveillance for two control buys. They tried to give me another one, but I did not serve her. The commonwealth did not play fair. Coming from DC and being Black, that was not a good look, not to mention my record. Basically, they looked at me as a known drug dealer. By just reading my rap sheet, they knew they had me by the balls. They were talking about six-years, nine-years probation. I was like, "Really, they must be tripping for real."

The streets had me washed up. Yes, especially the ones who hate your downfall. I wasn't even in three months, and they had me counted out already. I wasn't concerned about what I was hearing. I was the one who got to fight these people. I am going to tell you now that I was feeling really low with just the thought of what could happen. I was facing five to forty years in the state of Virginia. It was no question. I had to lace up my shoes and rumble.

CHAPTER 16

I kept trying to find a way to rumble these people. They had the drugs in the lab report. Also, they had a highly trained detective with a sworn testimony. Virginia would bring up charges you caught thirty years ago. They had that against me, and I was on probation for a federal case. It wasn't looking good. I had to wake up every day, dealing with what I saw. This shit was depressing. Everything was about food and kitchen shit. Dudes could not even get out on a $1,000 bond, which was 10 percent $100. What the fuck am I doing here? You can tell I was really getting frustrated being here. Something had to give. Months went by. I tried to see what else they might be holding back on. I wasn't dealing with anybody here but her. She was the only one. Her record was fucked up as well—drug attic and known prostitute, which I did not know about. This was crazy. She was responsible for a lot of convictions out here in Arlington. She walked the streets every day like she did not do shit. I found that out from the dude who knew her. Now that was some crazy shit. They didn't care out here. They would ask, "Who got you?" I could feel they did the same thing as well before. I could see in their faces. The only thing they could say was, "That's fucked up."

Now that I had been here. I saw which type of individuals I was around. Maybe two people in the whole unit have a drug charge. Most are here for violations, petty crimes, really. I know myself. I did not want to take my anger out on anyone. It was not their fault. I was here. I was worried about what I had to deal with. I was not worried about what was on my tray. "Are you going to eat it or not?" This shit was crazy. Nobody has a concern in the world. It was like a rehab/shelter. I could not believe I put myself through this again. I was trying to find an angel I could use. Entrapment was a good one. I was called to come out here. The commonwealth always has another case to justify for the one you are trying to fight. Another route was the credibility of the informant who sent me up. It was case law on that as well. The government does not have to reveal your accuser for their safety. It was always something. There is a lot of bullshit with them always coming up with why you might not be able to use this case of law, basically wanting you to give up fighting. The commonwealth has its own law. The justice system for a Black man in America—point blank period!

That was when I made up my mind that it was over for me almost fifty years old. I've been fighting a drug case and been around dudes that didn't give a fuck about anything. I just wanted to get out to sell more goods to get high, not going to throw my life away like that. God kept giving me warnings to the point that he had to really show me. I had to go through this to really see the big picture. I could have lost my life from drinking and smoking. I could have lost it because someone might have thought I really had some real money because of my lifestyle. That's why I stressed that I am truly blessed. At my age, I am even blessed to have a support system. God is really good. That is why I thank Joe for giving me the encouragement to write this book.

It was getting near my trial date. We were ready for trial because the offer never changed to six years with nine years probation. I was not going to take that on the day of trial. The government was not ready. The prosecutor went into early labor. Her water broke, and my lawyer really argued for dismissal. They could have gotten another prosecutor to handle the case. Also, she knew she was close to having her baby. The judge gave the government the benefit of the doubt just because her water broke early. That was crazy Virginia. So they gave us another trial date.

Your second drug conviction is a mandatory three years in Virginia; your third one is ten years. I was already in fourteen months. I saw they were not playing fair at all. I knew if I lost in the trial. They were going to give me the high in. On what I was facing for five to forty years, my lawyer said, "If I can get you a good deal, would you take it?"

I said, "It all depends on the probation time."

He came back with an offer of five years—three years mandatory and two on probation. Now if they came with this, it let me know they are not ready for trial. Should I take the plea? I already had fourteen months and two years of probation. I couldn't get anything better than that. One year of being out, I could put in for termination of my probation just on good behavior. So I took the offer. I was not trying to risk my chances of blowing trial. Honestly, that was the shortest. I would have been locked up. That is why I say I am blessed. It was God's doing. It made me lay down for a minute like a child being punished for a while. Now I know my purpose. This is my redemption.

CHAPTER 17

Being here, I've seen dudes were alive but were not living out there. Also, without the same morals and principles I was talking about early in the book, I could tell they would have done the same thing. Just like the woman who got me here in the first place, it was like the land of the dead. Hearing and seeing, they just wanted to get out by all means necessary just to get high all over again. Mental health is at an all-time high in society. So many are on medication just to escape the realities of responsibilities.

These are the same individuals and society that I've walked past or driven past every day. I was not really concerned about them because it was not me. It really hit home now. I asked myself, *Do you want to be a part of the problem?* Man up and be a part of the solution. So many of our people are lost men and women, starting from the young to the old. Again, how can a nineteen-year-old be homeless? No one wants to put their signature on paper so they can get released. They don't even care if he rots in jail. That is really sad. That is what I see every day of being here. More came through the door, sliding in. That is why I called it a rehab shelter. It is a nightmare for me for real.

God wanted me to go through this to understand his plan for me, being around guys old enough to be your father and grandfather still breaking the law at almost fifty years old. The chances I took. Getting five years is a blessing. Three mandatory into probation. Due to the circumstances, I couldn't ask for anything better. It is truly a blessing. I had too many chances. I cannot keep playing with my life. So I am telling you the game is over. For my age, I have seen a lot at an early age, still here sharing my story with you. I must have angels walking with me every day. I never had drug addiction problems and never experienced homelessness burnt my bridges with anyone. I am proud to say that. That is why I have to turn my life around. It is not going to be easy, just keeping it real. My lifestyle alone can be a problem. I like nice things and living life. I just have to be patient and wait for my turn. Everything takes time. That is why I am doing everything now to be prepared for my return. I do not have a pride problem; if I need some assistance this go-round, the saying goes, "It's never too late."

Now that I am a part of the solution. I am going to join the brotherhood of saving Black brothers and sisters. I have buddies playing their part to this day. Now it is my turn. I am starting a nonprofit organization called Operation Hope: Helping Other People Excel. It is a lifeline to let returning citizens know we are here for them. Do you not like using the term *ex-cons*? We are citizens returning back to society. My goal is to provide some basic assistance for returning citizens to help build self-worth and confidence, achieve success, and find a positive path. We offer some resources needed to start over from nothing, like transportation resources like a SmarTrip card for job searches, clothing, shoes, and undergarments. Many returning citizens do not have a support system, which is needed when coming back to the communities. Many are coming back with mental health issues and with history of drug addictions. They are lacking self-worth and purpose. These men and women need signs of hope. "Helping other people excel" is just having someone who really cares. I have the understanding on what they are going through, which makes a big difference. Leading by example really tells a lot about your character.

I am willing, driven, and determined to be a part of this movement. Operation Hope is really needed, which is going to be on the front line for my brothers and sisters and be there with them for support as they returning back to the communities that they left. That is my goal and mission. I know what it is like firsthand myself. That is one of the reasons we return to prison so soon. God gave me the gift and ability to lead. That is what I am going to do—leading by example. All I can tell my brothers and sisters in the struggle is, "Hold on and be strong. You do not have to worry about anything. We are proud Black people!" These are words from the great Tupac.

CHAPTER 18

Sharing my life story of being a boy to a man was a journey. I was happy to share it with you. I would not take it back either. Sometimes I asked myself what if. What if my father was in my life? What if my mother would have waited to have us, giving her a chance to be financially stable? The point I am making is, who is to say how I would have turned out? A buddy of mine would always use this term. The qualities of life can make a difference and can hinder you as well. If children are not taught basic life skills, having a good upbringing would mean nothing. Everything starts from home. We passed down what we were taught. Who is to say that was right? Even when we went to school, everything was taught how another race saw it. Most of them were lies.

We need role models for the young ones and not just be there, spoiling them with materialistic things. Boys must be taught to become a man. Girls must be taught to become a woman. We must share with them the understanding of the two so they will always be able to stand firm on their own two feet. That is what we have been lacking as a race. We were taught to hate one another, keep each other down, do not respect our women. Our women are ashamed of who they are. We built so much hate toward one another. That is an ugly word to use—hate. White is supposed to be beautiful and pure, and Black is ugly, bad, and wicked.

Some things go hand in hand. Myself, for example—I was from the hood but was able to see outside the box. Some do not know anything about the ghettos. That environment really can have a hold on you. That is if you let it. Most never will see anything about that.

It is good to strive for you and your family so they can have a better way of life. You cannot forget where you came from as well. Basically, share with them the sacrifices you had to make so they are able to benefit from your labor.

Nothing in life is free. As people, we need more leaders. I have heard this for so long. I do not fuck with the youngins. They keep doing dumb shit. I do not fuck with the old heads. They think they know everything. Truth be told, we all play a part. We were young before. We just got older. The same goes for the young ones. I was just like the youth. So how can I turn my back on them? For someone my age, I'll think twice about it. You should already know. Been there and done that. It all goes back to leading by example. Young or old, it does not matter. If you have anything to share, give it up. Do not be selfish and hold onto it. That is why we are lacking as people. Each one should teach one.

Everything I shared with you was the truth. Some might be upset with me for giving you some games for free. Everything in life is not about profit. Even before now, I always gave games away. Some would say the game is to be sold, not told. That is bullshit to me. That is being selfish. You are keeping it to yourself. Soon, the ones who are really hungry are going to blow past your hating ass and see you for who you really are. They are the worst individuals to be around. They are in a good space. They do not want to share knowledge to help someone else. They always want you to need them for something. You see, that's why I am glad I went through what I did; you cannot tell me bullshit. That's where I am today. I did not have to go to jail to know myself. Most things I learned at an early age in life. Given forever, I want to get back on a positive note this time. Who is better to let someone know their worth? That goes for young or old. I am the struggle! I hope you got something out of my testimony. I am the voice. To all the ones who did not understand the sacrifices made by others for another, you never know what a person did to make sure someone else was all right. That goes for your parents, children, your woman, and also for close friends that you have love for. Everybody wants the benefits but not the sacrifices. I asked you, would you have done it?

ACKNOWLEDGMENTS

First, I would like to thank God, the creator of all living.

To my grandmother, Frances Whitting (RIP).

To my great-great-aunt, Amanda Berry (RIP).

To my great-great-uncle, Carlton Berry (RIP).

To my mother, Gloria Minor.

To my father, Charlie Morton

To my stepmother, Shirl Morton.

To my siblings, Toye, Tye', Li'l Butch. May y'all rest in peace.

To JC Whitney JR, Cassandra. Big sis we all we got!

To my nieces and nephews.

To all my closest friends, Joe, Mona, Freak, Boe, Shawn, Ray, Day Day, and Big Sam Boe.

If I did not mention you, it is no love lost. To the females that were with me with my struggles, you know who you are.

Special thanks go out to Tarsha Brooks, my next-door neighbor. I remember you riding the bus and coming to see me down Lorton when everyone else left me for dead. I could never forget you, girl. You will always be in my heart.

Special, special thanks to all my haters! You are the best. I could not have done it without you.

____

This journey starts with an inner-city youth growing up. His journey started at an early age, and he was once lost. He found his purpose in life transitioning from a boy to a man.